W9-CNR-101

Animal Habitats

The Swan on the Lake

Text by Jennifer Coldrey

**Photographs by
Oxford Scientific Films**

RS OD MT TS MC FM
Gareth Stevens Publishing
Milwaukee

Where swans live

Swans are water birds. They like to live on open stretches of still water. You can find them on ponds, lakes, canals, reservoirs, and even on flooded areas of land. Some also live on slow-moving rivers, while others may be found in the salt water of harbors and estuaries and even out at sea. In winter, especially, many swans move from freshwater lakes and rivers to a seacoast. They take shelter in bays and estuaries, where the water is less likely to freeze. Swans often gather in large flocks during the winter.

A lake is an ideal place for swans to live, providing it has plenty of plants and other small *aquatic* animals for the birds to eat. The water must not be too deep, or the swans will be unable to reach the bottom to find food. The best kind of lake has gently sloping sides (not steep banks) which allow the birds to get in and out of the water easily, and the young to scramble onto land. Small bays or inlets with shallow water up to 3 feet (1 m) deep are useful places of shelter for swans with a young family.

A family of Mute Swans rests quietly at the edge of the lake where they live.

A group of swans rides across the choppy water on a cold winter day.

The plants growing in and around the edges of a lake are very important to the swans. They provide a good supply of nest material, while the tall reeds and rushes are a marvelous place of shelter, especially for the young *cygnets*. Swans are sometimes found on land, when they come out of the water to graze in fields. But they always nest close to the lakeside and are never far from the water.

Mute Swans, also known as European Swans, often spend the whole year on the same lake. Other swans, especially those living in very cold climates, have to leave their summer homes before the winter sets in. The lakes they nest in freeze over, and the birds have to travel long distances to find an open stretch of water where they can feed and live throughout the winter. The following spring they return to the same lakes to breed.

3

Mute Swans look very graceful as they sail along on the water.

The Mute Swan

The Mute, or European, Swan is one of the world's best-known swans. It is quite tame and is often found on lakes, both in the town and in the country. It is easy to see as it sails along majestically on the water. The Mute Swan is a large white bird, up to 5 feet (1.6 m) long from the tip of its bill to the end of its tail. It has big, powerful wings, which span 6 or 7 feet (2-2½ m) when they are fully spread. The long neck, with its thick feathers, is usually held in a graceful curve. The beak is a bright orange-red, tipped with a black nail, and at the base, close to the nostrils, is a large black, fleshy knob. This knob is bigger in the male swan (called a *cob*) than in the female (called a *pen*). In other ways, the male and female are similar, although the cob is slightly bigger than the pen. Both have large black, webbed feet.

The Mute Swan is so-named because it is nearly silent or mute. It never calls at night, as other swans do. However, it does make some noises, including various grunts, hisses, and snorts, and, when it flies, its beating wings make a wonderful singing throb which can be heard a long way off.

The Mute Swan is now found in many parts of the world. People have always admired its grace and beauty and have taken it from Europe to live on lakes and ponds in other parts of the world. It has now been introduced to Australia, New Zealand, parts of North America, and South Africa. But its natural home is in various parts of Europe and Asia, and here there are flocks of truly wild birds. In parts of the Soviet Union and China the swans *migrate* to warmer places further south during the winter. But most Mute Swans do not migrate. They stay in much the same place the whole year round, even though flocks of young birds may move to different areas to find food and space.

Mute Swans are quite tame and even semi-domesticated in some countries. In England they are often known as royal birds. This is because, many centuries ago, all Mute Swans were owned by the King. They were captured and kept by special swan-herders or keepers, whose job it was to clip the swans' wings so they could not fly away. Later, the king allowed certain noblemen and other important people to own flocks of swans. In those days, swans were considered good eating, and a lot of poaching, or stealing, went on. The birds were therefore marked so that owners could recognize their own swans. Some had nicks cut into their bills, while others had their feet tagged or marked in some way. Even today, there are two old London clubs that own and mark swans on the river Thames, and some swans still belong to the Queen of England.

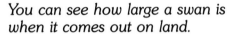

You can see how large a swan is when it comes out on land.

A Whooper Swan.

Other white swans

Four other kinds of large white swan live in the northern hemisphere. During the summer they nest and rear their young on lakes in the far north, some even inside the Arctic Circle. Later in the year, they fly south to warmer places to spend the winter.

Whooper Swans breed mainly in Iceland, northern Scandinavia, Russia, and parts of Siberia. In winter, they migrate south to countries like Great Britain and other parts of Europe and Asia, where they find food and shelter in lakes, marshes, and estuaries. The Whooper Swan is about the same size as the Mute Swan, but it has a straighter neck and longer wings (needed for flying long distances). Its bill is black and yellow. The Whooper Swan has a loud whooping call, which gives it its name.

The head and neck of a Bewick's Swan.

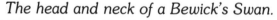

The head of a Whistling Swan.

Bewick's Swans are like a smaller version of the Whooper Swan. They are 4 feet (1.2 m) long from the bill to the end of the tail. The yellow patch on their bills is not as long as the Whooper's, and they have a softer, more musical call. Bewick's Swans breed very far north on the arctic *tundra* of northern Russia and Siberia. They travel well over a thousand miles to spend the winter in northwestern Europe or in parts of southeast Asia.

Trumpeter and Whistling, or North American, Swans both live and breed in the far north of the United States and Canada. The Whistling Swan is very similar to the Bewick's Swan, but it only has a tiny speck of yellow on its bill. It has a high-pitched whistling call, but it also makes a soft, trumpeting sound.

The Trumpeter is the largest and most impressive of all the swans, with a body up to 6 feet (1.8 m) long. It has a wedge-shaped head with a totally black bill (apart from a trace of orange on the underside). It has a loud, deep trumpeting call. Trumpeter Swans are now quite rare and are only found in Alaska and other small areas of the northwest United States and northwest Canada. Unlike Whistling Swans, which migrate long distances for the winter, most Trumpeters stay in the same place all year round.

A Trumpeter Swan from the Pacific Northwest.

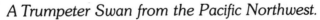

The Black Swan from Australia has crinkled, curly feathers.

Swans from the south

Not all swans are white. There are black swans in Australia, and some have now been introduced into New Zealand. Black Swans are common on many lakes in Australia and are often found in large colonies, sometimes as many as 50,000 birds in one flock.

The Black Swan is a handsome creature. About the same size as the Mute Swan, it has very dark feathers, black with dark brownish tinges. The feathers close to the body are paler, but otherwise the *plumage* is completely black, except for a broad white band along the back edge of each wing. This shows up very clearly when the birds fly. Black Swans have dark grey legs and feet. The bill is red with a white band near the tip. The males and females look alike. Although not as noisy as most other swans, Black Swans make a high-pitched bugling call, as well as other sounds.

Two other types of swan live in southern parts of South America. One is the Black-necked Swan, a beautiful bird about 48 inches (1.3 m) long with a snow-white body and a long black neck. It has pink legs and feet and a blue bill with a large red knob at the base. The Black-necked Swan makes a weak, high-pitched call which sounds much like a toy trumpet.

These Black-necked Swans have a young cygnet to look after.

The other is the Coscoroba Swan. This is a small white bird with a shortish neck, more like a goose than a swan. Its plumage is white except for black tips to the wings. It has pink legs and feet and a bright red bill which is flatter and more duck-like than the beaks of other swans. It makes a goose-like call.

Black-necked and Coscoroba Swans are sometimes found together on the same lake. They breed in southern South America, in countries such as Tierra del Fuego, the Falkland Islands, Chile, Argentina, Paraguay, Uruguay, and southern Brazil. Many move further north to spend the winter in warmer places.

The Coscoroba Swan looks more like a goose than a swan.

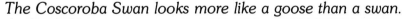

The swan's body

Swans are large and sturdy. Their bodies are broad and boat-shaped, narrowing to a wedge-shaped tail. Their streamlined shape helps them move easily through the water.

A swan's legs are short and stumpy. The feet are very large, with webs of skin between the toes. The swan uses its feet like paddles, to push itself along in the water. The legs are set far back on the body. This helps in swimming and gives the swan power to push against the water and to tip its body forward so that the tail sticks up vertically out of the water. This is called "upending." Swans use their long necks to probe underwater and find food. They can reach even further when they are upending.

One swan paddles forward, while the other "upends" to find food below.

Feathers fly as these two swans preen and rearrange their plumage.

The feathers covering the body help keep a swan warm and dry. This is especially important to a water bird. Close to the skin is a layer of soft, fluffy down which keeps the bird's body extra cozy. Like most other birds, swans spend a lot of time cleaning and rearranging their feathers. They keep them waterproof by smearing them with oil produced from a special *gland* at the base of the tail. The oil is picked up when the swan rubs its beak on the gland and then combs it through the feathers, one by one. This is called *preening*.

Once a year, during the summer, a swan loses its feathers and grows a new set. This is called *molting*. It happens in stages, the wing and tail feathers molting before the body feathers. While the wing feathers are molting, the swans are unable to fly. During this time, they need to find a safe place to rest. Young birds usually join together in large flocks to molt. Older birds with young stay near their nest, and the female usually molts before the male.

Swans have quite good eyesight. They can see movements on either side of the body without having to turn their heads. However, they cannot see very clearly straight ahead, and they sometimes bump into things when they are flying.

As this swan comes in to land, it pushes its feet forward to help it brake.

Movement on land and in the air

Swans glide gracefully on the water, but they are very clumsy on land. Their broad webbed feet help them walk on soft, slippery mud and also on ice, but they can only waddle along slowly, swaying awkwardly from side to side.

It is quite a different thing to see them flying. Swans have big, strong wings. They fly majestically, with slow, powerful wingbeats, their necks outstretched and their feet tucked up under their bodies. They use their tails to help them steer. As they come down to land, their feet come forward to help them brake and they spread out their tail feathers. Because they are large and heavy, swans find it difficult both to land and take off. When taking off, they need a runway of at least 20-30 yards (20-30 m) to get up enough speed. They run along, either on the ground or pattering on the surface of the water, facing into the wind and flapping their wings madly to help lift them off into the air.

Swans often fly over long distances — up to 1000 miles (1600 km) or more — when they migrate. They usually travel in family groups, sometimes within a larger flock, and often in a V-formation or in a diagonal line. They call to each other frequently, which helps keep them together on their long journey. Migrating swans travel mainly at night, using the daytime to stop and feed. They prefer to fly in clear weather when they can use the position of the sun or stars to guide them. Some swans have to migrate across the sea, where they cannot stop for food. The Whoopers that come to Great Britain from Iceland have to fly at least 500 miles (800 km) across the North Atlantic Ocean without stopping.

Migrating swans fly fast, at speeds between 30 and 50 mph (50-80 kph). But they fly even faster if the wind is behind them, up to 70 mph (112 kph). In clear weather they fly quite high, between 2000 and 5000 feet (600-1500 m), or even higher, but in bad weather they stay closer to the gound. On small local flights they fly between 50 and several hundred feet (15-100 m) up in the air. It is always very exciting to see or hear a flock of swans flying overhead.

A Mute Swan in flight.

A Mute Swan uses its bill to dabble on the surface and pick up waterweeds.

Food and feeding

Swans feed mainly on water plants. They use their long necks to pull up weeds from the bottom of the lake, and when they upend, they are able to reach as deep as 3 feet (1 m) to find food. Swans eat the leaves, stems, roots, and seeds of many different water plants. They nibble at plants floating on the surface and also at those growing in marshy ground around the edges of the lake. Some swans eat small animals too — including insects, worms, snails, tadpoles, and tiny fish.

The swan uses its broad, flattened bill to scoop up food from the mud or from the water. On each side of the bill are fine comb-like fringes which catch and strain small pieces of food as the water is squeezed out of the mouth. The sharp edges of the bill and the nail at the tip help the swan to bite and tear off pieces of plant, while the tongue has a rough, spiny surface which helps to grasp and grind up food.

Swans, like other birds, do not have teeth. Instead, they swallow little pieces of grit and stone which grind up the food after it has been swallowed. The grit is stored in a special part of the stomach called the *gizzard.* This has strong, muscular walls and is the place where the food is broken down into fine pieces. It then passes on down the *intestine,* where the nutrition is absorbed into the body.

The edges of the bill have comb-like fringes which help the swan grasp and strain off food from the water.

Sometimes swans use their feet to paddle in the mud and break off pieces of plant which they pull to the surface. They often disturb and pull up far more food than they need. The leftovers are usually eaten by other water birds which sometimes gather around the feeding swans to wait for tidbits.

Swans sometimes come onto land to feed. This is more common in winter, when flocks of swans can be seen grazing in wet fields and meadows, on grass, and even on young crops. In autumn they like to eat leftovers from the harvest, such as spilled grain and broken pieces of turnip and potato.

Swans use their long necks to reach down to the bottom and pull up food.

Courtship and mating

Swans do not usually breed until they are 3 or 4 years old. But they look around for a mate when they are younger than this. They usually pair up during the autumn, ready to start a family the following spring.

The cobs become very fierce and aggressive when they are looking for a mate. They fight with each other and show off their handsome plumage to attract a pen. Once they have found a mate, they guard her jealously and will attack any other males that come anywhere near their *territory*.

Male Mute Swans put on a magnificent display when they are feeling angry or threatened. The cob will arch up his wings and ruffle the feathers on his neck, meanwhile laying his head and neck back onto his body. An intruder usually backs away in fear, but if he doesn't, the swan will attack, rushing forward with wings flapping and both feet pushing together against the water. Other swans have similar displays, but not all are as fierce and bad-tempered as the Mute Swan.

A courting pair of Mute Swans. The male, on the right, has ruffled up the feathers on his neck as part of his courtship display.

These two cobs are fighting viciously over the right to claim a territory.

Before mating, the pen and cob go through a special courtship display. In the Mute Swan, the two birds turn to face each other on the water. They move their heads from side to side, sometimes rubbing their necks together and even "kissing" with their bills. Now and again they dip their heads into the water and occasionally turn to rub their heads against their bodies. Finally the pen lowers her body into the water and the cob climbs on top of her. He passes his *sperm* into her body to *fertilize* the eggs. The two birds then rise up from the water, breast to breast, with necks outstretched. They waggle their heads from side to side and finally sink back into the water, where they bathe and preen and wag their tails.

Swans are very faithful birds. Once a pen and cob have mated and raised a family, they will usually stay together for life. A close bond builds up between the pair, and their partnership is strengthened by various displays and greeting ceremonies between them.

A female Mute Swan sitting on her large nest of reeds and sticks.

Nesting and laying eggs

Most wild swans nest in pairs, on their own, away from other birds. However, Black Swans are different. They nest close together in large colonies, with only 3 feet (1 m) or so between each nest. There are also places in England and parts of Europe where large flocks of semi-domesticated Mute Swans nest in colonies.

All swans build their nests close to water, often on the bank or on an island in the lake. A small island is a very good place because it is surrounded by water and cannot be reached by land *predators*. Many swans come back to nest in the same place year after year. Some even build on top of their old nest.

Nesting begins during spring or early summer. The cob generally chooses the spot and starts to gather material for building the nest. The nest is usually made of reeds, sedges, rushes, sticks, and sometimes moss. The cob passes the plant material back to the pen, who arranges it into a large round heap.

Swans' nests are enormous, sometimes as much as 9-12 feet (3-4 m) across at the bottom, and well over 3 feet (1 m) deep. The pen makes a shallow dip in the center, sometimes lining it with grass or a small amount of down and feathers which she plucks from her breast. The final nest is fairly floodproof (even if built in shallow water) and usually high enough above the water to be safe from enemies in the lake.

The pen lays her *clutch* of eggs, one every other day. Mute Swans usually lay between five and eight eggs. The eggs are oval, greenish-white in color, and about 4½ inches (11-12 cm) long. They soon become stained and dirty in the nest. Once all the eggs are laid, the pen sits on them to *incubate* them. She keeps them warm by fluffing up some of her feathers so that a patch of bare, warm skin on her belly presses against the eggs. Now and then she turns the eggs to make sure they are warmed evenly on all sides.

The cob stands guard nearby and chases off intruders. Occasionally he takes a turn at incubating the eggs while the pen goes off to feed. If both parents leave the nest, they cover the eggs with a layer of nest material to hide them.

The male stays nearby to guard the nest and to look after the pen as she sits on the eggs.

These newly hatched cygnets cluster under their mother's body for warmth and protection. Two eggs have not yet hatched.

The young cygnets

It takes five weeks for the eggs to hatch. Just before the chicks hatch, faint clicking sounds, followed by cheeping noises, can be heard from inside each egg. The parents can undoubtedly hear these sounds, and it is thought that the unborn chicks can also hear noises through their shells.

The chicks break out of their shells using a special sharp nail on the end of their beaks called an egg-tooth. This drops off a few days later. The chicks all hatch within two days. At first they are tired, wet, and bedraggled. But they soon dry off to become little bundles of fluffy grey down.

Young swans, or cygnets, are born with their eyes open. They are soon able to move about, and when only a day or two old, they will leave the nest and follow their parents into the water. They know instinctively how to swim. They peck at plants and insects in the water and learn what foods are good to eat. Their parents help them by stirring the mud and bringing up weeds and other tidbits from the bottom. Very soon the young cygnets learn to find food for themselves. But they still rely on their parents to protect them from danger. During the day, they stay close to their parents, while at night they return to the nest, where they are kept safe and warm beneath their mother's body.

Mute Swans look after their young by carrying them around on their backs.

The Mute, Black, and Black-necked Swans all have a special way of protecting their offspring. They allow the cygnets to ride on their backs, where the chicks stay safe and warm, snuggled between the parent's wings.

Young cygnets make a variety of soft or loud cheeping calls, depending on whether they are warm, sleepy, and well-fed, or cold, hungry, and frightened. The calls they make are an important way of keeping in touch with each other and with their parents. The adults react quickly to their cries and sometimes answer with a soft, low call.

The baby cygnets follow their parents and soon learn to find food for themselves.

The cygnets in this family are now just over one month old.

Growing up

As the cygnets get older, feathers start to grow in place of their down. They gradually change from fluffy grey to a soft greyish-brown plumage. By about 4½ months old, their wing feathers are well-developed and the cygnets are ready to fly. The time when a young bird first takes to the wing is called *fledging*. Swans from the far north take only 2-3 months to fledge. The Arctic summer is very short, and these young swans need to develop quickly so that they are ready to fly south with their parents in the autumn. Black Swan cygnets, on the other hand, take as long as six months to fledge.

Most cygnets stay with their parents during their first winter. They may move to another patch of water to find more food and shelter. Sometimes the family lives apart from other swans. But it is more usual for swans to gather in large groups during the winter. Swans that migrate long distances prepare for their journey by feeding avidly and putting on weight.

The stores of fat they build up in their bodies help them to survive for many days without food. Swans stay together in family groups on migration. In this way, the young birds are able to learn the route from their parents.

After their first winter, young swans usually leave their parents. In fact, they are often driven away by the adults, who are anxious to start another family. The cob is already becoming jealous of the young male swans and he gets more aggressive as their plumage becomes whiter. As they grow older, young white swans lose their grey and brown feathers, until, at about one year, they are completely white. Their bills also change color. In the Mute Swan, the young greyish bill turns to a muddy pink, and finally, at two years old, to bright orange-red. Until they are ready to breed, young swans gather together in large flocks for much of the year. They sometimes rejoin their parents and any new brothers and sisters during the winter.

The young Mute Swan in this picture is about six months old. It still has a greyish bill and a lot of greyish-brown feathers.

Enemies and other dangers

Swans are large, aggressive birds. They have very few enemies because they are well able to defend themselves from attack. If another animal does try to attack them, or threatens their young, they put on a very frightening display. They either raise or flap their wings, ruffle their neck feathers, and often hiss and snort. When attacking, they move forward quickly, pushing both feet together across the water and striking out with their wings and beak. They can seriously hurt and even kill other animals. Human beings are occasionally injured by swans and most animals learn to keep clear of them.

The main enemies of swans are the animals which attack their eggs and young. Hungry predators such as foxes, wolves, dogs, coyotes, otters, and mink will all kill nestling chicks whenever they get the chance. They will also take eggs from the nest, and in some parts of the world, gulls and other predatory birds are known to eat swans' eggs. There are dangers from the water too, where large fish, like pike, steal up from below to grab young cygnets swimming at the surface. Pike have even been known to drown adult swans by holding their heads underwater until they die.

An angry Mute Swan raises its wings and moves quickly across the water to chase away an intruder.

The swan uses its wings and beak to attack an enemy. This small dog might easily get hurt.

The cygnets suffer from other dangers, too. Many of them die from cold, hunger, or disease. In fact, about half the total number of chicks that hatch die before they are three months old, and many more die before the end of their first winter. Not all the eggs hatch, either. If the nest becomes flooded, the eggs are likely to get chilled and the chicks inside will die.

All in all, very few swans grow up and manage to live long enough to breed. But among those that do, the healthy ones may live as long as fifteen years or more.

Swans sometimes die from accidents in the air. They frequently fly into overhead wires which they do not see ahead of them, and they occasionally bump into trees, bridges, or buildings, especially in bad weather. They sometimes land on wet roads, mistaking them for rivers. When this happens they are often killed or injured by traffic.

A large pike lurks in the water of the lake. Any small cygnets floating on the surface may well be in danger.

These two swans are not afraid of these fishermen. Fishermen only harm swans if they leave lead weights, hooks, and nylon lines behind in the lake.

Humans as enemies

Human beings are unfortunately among the worst enemies of swans. In the past, people shot swans regularly for meat. They also collected the down for stuffing quilts and pillows, while the large feathers were used for quill pens. In England and Europe, Mute Swans were semi-domesticated and kept mainly for eating, but many wild swans were killed, too. During the 19th century, the Mute Swan was completely exterminated in parts of Europe, while in North America, the Trumpeter Swan nearly became *extinct* because of shooting. Fortunately this shooting is now banned, and special laws protect most swans in the wild places where they live. Egg collecting has always been a threat to swans, and even today people steal or damage eggs, even though egg collecting is illegal in many countries.

People also harm swans by destroying or disturbing their *habitat,* so that the birds move away or are unable to breed. Marshland is often drained to make the land suitable for growing crops, and this means that water birds cannot live there any more. Noisy boats on lakes and rivers often upset the wildlife and *pollute* the water with oil and motor fuel. Other poisons come into the water from factories or from *pesticides* which are sprayed onto the land by foresters and farmers. These poisons find their way into the rivers and are washed down into lakes or out to the sea.

Mute Swans are especially affected by many of these dangers because they often live close to humans. Many Mute Swans are dying because of lead pollution in our waters. Some of the lead comes from scattered lead shot left behind by people shooting wildfowl, but swans are most affected by fishermen's lead weights which are dropped into the water or left on the bank after a day's fishing. Swans pick up this lead and use it like grit to grind up the food in their gizzards. The poison is soon absorbed into the body and the swans become ill and die.

Swans get hurt and tangled up in nylon fishing lines and hooks which careless fishermen leave behind on the bank. They can also be harmed by plastic bags or pieces of broken glass which become entwined in the weeds after people have thrown them away.

The cygnet in the center of this picture is suffering from lead poisoning. You can tell because it cannot hold its neck up straight.

A large number of geese and other water birds have gathered on this lake. Here they will find food and shelter during the winter.

Friends and neighbors

Many other water birds live and nest both on and around the edges of a lake. Ducks such as the Mallard, Teal, and Shoveler, dabble around on the surface and hunt for food near the edge of the water. Diving ducks, such as the Pochard and the Tufted Duck, swim and dive further out in deeper water. Geese are also common, especially in winter, when large numbers of water birds gather on sheltered lakes and other stretches of water. Canada Geese are common on many lakes. Like swans, they build their large nests near the water, often on islands, and they sometimes compete with swans for the best spots.

Other birds living on lakes include coots and moorhens, divers, grebes, pelicans, and even cormorants. Coots are especially common on large lakes and reservoirs. They spend a lot of time out on the open water, where they dive for weeds beneath the surface. Divers and grebes are expert fishermen. They dive down deep to catch fish, which they stab with their sharp beaks.

Many of these water birds nest among the reeds and rushes around the edges of the lake. Other birds visit the lake only to find food. Swifts, swallows, and martins come to hunt for insects over the surface of the water in the summer. Terns, kingfishers, and ospreys may visit the lake to plunge-dive for fish, while bitterns and herons wade in the shallows, looking for fishes, frogs, and other small animals to stab and eat. Herons sometimes eat baby birds, and they can therefore be a threat to swans with very young cygnets.

The Great Crested Grebe builds a nest like a floating platform. It is made out of water plants and is firmly attached to reeds or rushes at the edge of the lake.

Other animals including water voles, otters, muskrats, and beavers live by lakes and make their homes either in or close to the water. Swans are sometimes very hostile to these animals, even though voles, beavers, and muskrats do swans no harm. Swans are not very sociable, especially in the breeding season, when they will fight to protect their territories and young. They will attack other water birds that come too close and have even been known to go for cattle coming down to drink at the water's edge.

However, swans do not usually attack unless they are threatened by a real enemy. Providing there is plenty of food and space, they manage to live quite happily with their neighbors on the lake.

The American Beaver lives in lakes and ponds of Canada and the northern U.S., where it is a neighbor of both Trumpeter and Whistling Swans.

Life on the lake

Swans are mainly plant-eaters. Many other water birds feed on plants in the lake, too. But each different kind of bird feeds in a different way, either on different plants, or in a different part of the lake. So, although there is competition, there is usually plenty of food for all.

We can see this more clearly by drawing a diagram to show the different ways in which swans and other water birds find their food. Swans can feed in deeper water than many other birds on the lake. When upending, they can reach to about 3 feet (1 m), deeper than any of the geese or surface-feeding ducks. Diving ducks, like the Tufted and Pochard, can, on the other hand, dive down as far as 12 feet (4 m) to find food. They can therefore feed on different water plants and animals which others cannot reach. In the shallow water around the edges of a lake there is usually plenty of plant life for dabbling ducks, waders, swans, and other birds to find enough to eat. Swans do not eat fish, so there is no competition between them and fish-eating birds like herons, divers, and grebes.

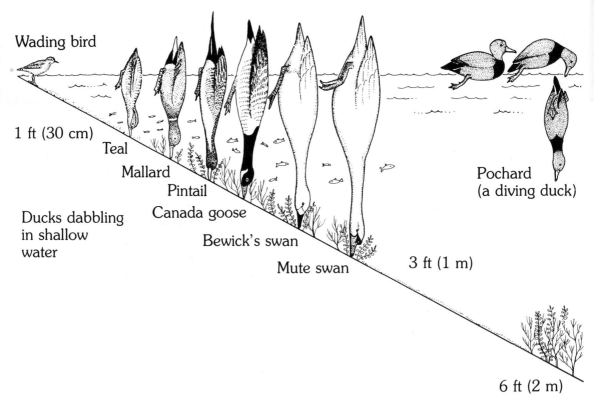

Wading bird

1 ft (30 cm)
Teal
Mallard
Pintail
Ducks dabbling in shallow water
Canada goose
Bewick's swan
Mute swan
3 ft (1 m)
Pochard (a diving duck)
6 ft (2 m)

Depth at which different water birds find food.

This peaceful lake provides a perfect home for this pair of Mute Swans.

Lakes with plenty of food, shelter, and shallow stretches of water make a perfect place for swans to live. But swans need clean water and plenty of peace and quiet, too. Unfortunately, human beings have already done much to harm swans and the wild places where they live. But many people are now trying to put things right by protecting wild areas of lake and marshland and by making new lakes and reservoirs where swans and other water birds can live safely and happily. Swans are among the most beautiful and graceful birds in the world. It is up to us to look after their needs, so that we will always be able to see them on our lakes.

Glossary

These new words about swans appear in the text in *italics*, just as they appear here.

aquatic . . . . living in water
clutch . . . . a set of eggs
cob . . . . a male swan
cygnet. . . . . a young swan
extinct. . . . . no longer existing
fertilize . . . . to join a male sperm with a female's egg, so that a new individual can grow from the fertilized egg
fledging . . . . taking the first flight
gizzard . . . . part of a swan's stomach, with strong muscular walls for grinding up food
gland . . . . a part of the body which produces a special substance such as oil or sweat
habitat . . . . the natural home of any plant or animal
incubate. . . . . . . to keep (eggs) warm so that they will hatch
intestine . . . . part of the gut (digestive system) below the stomach

molting . . . . shedding the feathers in order to replace them with new ones
migrate . . . . move to a different area at different times of year, either for breeding or wintering
pen . . . . a female swan
pesticides . . . . . . poisonous chemicals used to kill pests, especially insects
plumage . . . . the body covering (feathers) of a bird
pollution. . . . . . . damage caused to the air,
(pollute) water and earth, from dirt, rubbish, and poisons left by people
predator . . . . an animal that kills and eats other animals
preening. . . . . . . cleaning and oiling the feathers with the bill
sperm . . . . (short for spermatozoa) male sex cells
territory . . . . piece of land or water which an animal defends against intruders
tundra. . . . . treeless regions of the Arctic where the ground below the surface is permanently frozen

Reading level analysis: SPACHE 3.7, FRY 5, FLESCH 76 (fairly easy), RAYGOR 4, FOG 6, SMOG 4

Library of Congress Cataloging-in-Publication Data

Coldrey, Jennifer. The swan on the lake.
(Animal habitats)
Summary: Text and illustrations depict swans feeding, breeding, and defending themselves in their natural habitats.
1. Swans — juvenile literature. [1. Swans] I. Oxford Scientific Films. II. Title. III. Series.
QL696.A52C65   1986   598.4'1   86-5719
ISBN 1-55532-091-0
ISBN 1-55532-066-X (lib. bdg.)

North American edition first published in 1987 by
Gareth Stevens, Inc.
7221 West Green Tree Road   Milwaukee, WI 53223, USA.
Text copyright © 1987 by Oxford Scientific Films.
Photographs copyright © 1987 by Oxford Scientific Films.

Conceived, designed, and produced by Belitha Press Ltd., London.

Typeset by Ries Graphics ltd., Milwaukee.
Printed in Hong Kong by South China Printing Co.
U.S. Editors: MaryLee Knowlton & Mark J. Sachner.
Art Director: Treld Bicknell.   Design: Naomi Games.
Line drawings: Lorna Turpin.
Scientific Consultants: Gwynne Vevers and David Saintsing.

Photography: **Oxford Scientific Films Ltd.** for pp. 4, 5, 18, 24, 31, and *front cover* (photographer G.I. Bernard): p. 22 and title page (photographer Alastair Shay); pp. 2, 12, and *back cover* (photographer David Cayless); pp. 3, 10, 15 *above*, 19, 25 *below*, 26, and 28 (photographer David Thompson); p. 6 both (photographer J.B. Blossom); pp. 7 *above* and 9 *below* (photographer Peter O'Toole); p. 7 *below* (photographer Margot Conte); p. 8 (photographer J.A.L. Cooke); p. 9 *above* (photographer H.W. Price); pp. 11, 14, 15 *below*, and 21 *below* (photographers David and Sue Cayless); p. 13 (photographer Barry Walker); pp. 16 and 21 *above* (photographer Mike Birkhead); p. 17 (photographer Martyn Chillmaid); pp. 20 and 23 (photographer Richard Packwood); pp. 25 *above* and 27 (photographer C.M. Perrins); p. 29 *above* (photographer D.J. Saunders); p. 29 *below* (photographer Harry Engels).

32